08/2

D0056200

The American Mosaic
Immigration Today

Famous Immigrants and Their Stories

Sara Howell

PowerKiDS
press™

New York

Published in 2015 by The Rosen Publishing Group, Inc.
29 East 21st Street, New York, NY 10010

First Edition

Editors: Jennifer Way and Norman D. Graubart
Book Design: Andrew Povolny
Photo Research: Katie Stryker

Photo Credits: Cover Handout/Getty Images; p. 5 Greg Nelson/Sports
Illustrated/Getty Images; p. 6 Kean Collection/Archive Photos/Getty
Images; p. 7 Justin Sullivan/Getty Images; p. 8 Hulton Archive/Getty
Images; p. 9 Archive Holdings Inc./Getty Images; p. 10 Transcendental
Graphics/Archive Photos/Getty Images; p. 11 James Steidl/Shutterstock.
com; p. 12 Apic/Hulton Archive/Getty Images; p. 13 (top) Universal
Images Group/Getty Images; p. 13 (bottom) Baltimore Sun/McClatchy-
Tribune/Getty Images; pp. 15 (top and bottom), 18 Bloomberg/Getty
Images; p. 16 Pascal Le Segretain/Getty Images; p. 17 (top) Amanda
Edwards/Getty Images; p. 17 (bottom) Venturelli/Getty Images; p. 19
Mike Coppola/Getty Images; p. 20 Otto Greule Jr/Getty Images; p. 21
(top) Robert Prezioso/Getty Images; p. 21 (bottom) Rick Stewart/Getty
Images; p. 22 Kevin Mazur/WireImage/Getty Images.

Library of Congress Cataloging-in-Publication Data

Howell, Sara.
  Famous immigrants and their stories / by Sara Howell. — First edition.
    pages cm. — (The American mosaic : immigration today)
  Includes index.
  ISBN 978-1-4777-6750-4 (library binding) — ISBN 978-1-4777-6751-1
  (pbk.) – ISBN 978-1-4777-6652-1 (6-pack)
  1. Immigrants—United States—History—Juvenile literature. 2. Immigrants
—United States—Biography—Juvenile literature. 3. United States—
Emigration and immigration—History—Juvenile literature. I. Title.
  JV6450.H69 2015
  305.9'06912092273—dc23
                                        2014004866

Manufactured in the United States of America

CPSIA Compliance Information: Batch #WS14PK1: For Further Information contact Rosen
Publishing, New York, New York at 1-800-237-9932

Contents

Our Changing Culture

Has your family ever moved from one place to another? Many people move to different cities or states for work or to be close to family members. Some people even move to new countries! People who move from one country to another are called **immigrants**.

Immigrants play an important role in American **culture**. They have made scientific discoveries, set sports records, and started businesses. They bring their own cultures, music, food, art, and language with them. There are about 40 million immigrants living in the United States today. Each year about 1 million more arrive. New immigrants keep our country's culture growing and changing!

Manu Ginóbili (front) was born in Argentina. He has played basketball for the San Antonio Spurs since 2002.

A Nation of Immigrants

Among the first American settlers were the Pilgrims, who settled in modern-day Massachusetts. The Pilgrims came from England.

Before the United States was a country, groups of Native Americans lived throughout North America. The first European settlers arrived and built homes and cities. Eventually American colonists formed a new country, the United States. Because almost all Americans have come from elsewhere, the United States is often called a nation of immigrants.

Most immigrants who come to the United States have permission to live and work here. They are called **permanent residents**. Those here without permission are called **undocumented immigrants**. Some immigrants, called **refugees**, come because they are not safe in their home countries.

Jose Antonio Vargas is an undocumented immigrant living in America. He gives speeches about how hard life is for undocumented immigrants.

Waves of Immigration

Over time, large waves, or groups, of immigrants have moved to the United States. The first wave was made up mostly of people from England, Germany, the Netherlands, and other countries in western Europe. These early colonists arrived between the 1600s and the start of the American Revolution. The next wave of immigrants began to arrive around 1820 and continued until 1870. These immigrants were also from western and northern Europe. About a third were from Ireland.

Franz Sigel was born in Germany. He became a major general in the US Army. He and other immigrants fought in many important battles in the Civil War.

These eastern European immigrants are arriving in New York. The Statue of Liberty is in the background.

A third wave of immigration took place between the 1880s and the 1920s. Many of these immigrants came from countries in southern and eastern Europe.

Today's Immigrants

Beginning in the 1920s, the US government set limits on the number of immigrants who could come to the United States each year. These laws, along with the Great Depression of the 1930s, caused fewer immigrants to come. In 1965, some of the immigration laws were **amended**, or changed. The number of immigrants arriving in the United States began to go back up.

The Great Depression lasted for over 10 years. Immigrants who came to America to find work could not find a job easily.

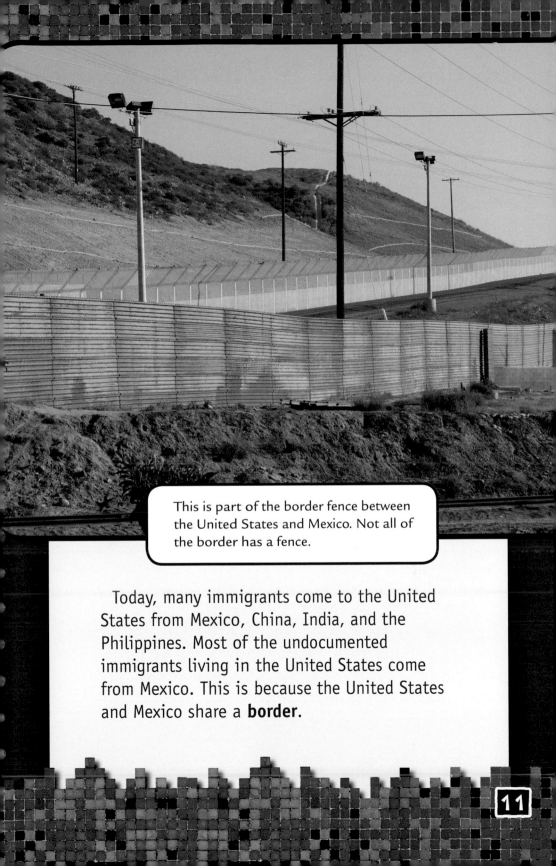

This is part of the border fence between the United States and Mexico. Not all of the border has a fence.

Today, many immigrants come to the United States from Mexico, China, India, and the Philippines. Most of the undocumented immigrants living in the United States come from Mexico. This is because the United States and Mexico share a **border**.

Science and Technology

Kalpana Chawla graduated from both the University of Texas and the University of Colorado.

Immigrants have made huge **contributions** to the fields of science and **technology**. Many move to the United States to study at universities and choose to stay. Ahmed Zewail was born in Egypt and came to the United States to study chemistry. He was awarded the Nobel Prize for Chemistry in 1999. Kalpana Chawla, the first Indian American astronaut, also came to the United States to study. In 1997, she became the first Indian woman in space.

Albert Einstein (1879–1955)

Albert Einstein was born in Ulm, Germany. He moved to America in 1933 and became an American citizen in 1940. He and other scientists designed the atomic bomb during World War II. Einstein worked and taught at Princeton University from 1933 to 1955, when he died.

Alfredo Quiñones-Hinojosa entered the United States from Mexico as an undocumented immigrant. Though he spoke no English, he went on to become a US **citizen** and is now a well-known doctor and author.

Alfredo Quiñones-Hinojosa (right) is a neurosurgeon, or a doctor who operates on people's brains.

Business Innovators

Immigrants often bring new ideas, start businesses, and create new products. In fact, blue jeans were first made and sold by a German immigrant named Levi Strauss.

Lowell Hawthorne, an immigrant from Jamaica, came to the United States when he was 21. Along with his family, he started the Golden Krust Caribbean Bakery & Grill, which sells traditional Jamaican foods.

An immigrant who has had great financial success in the United States is Sergey Brin. He left Russia with his family when he was six years old. He went on to study computer science and cofounded Google, one of the most valuable companies in the world!

Sergey Brin is wearing Google Glass in this photo. Google Glass is one of Google's many products.

Indra Nooyi
(1955–)

Indra Nooyi is the CEO of PepsiCo. PepsiCo is the second-largest food and beverage company in the world. Nooyi was born in Chennai, India, and went to Yale University. After graduating, Nooyi worked at Johnson & Johnson, Motorola, and several other companies. Nooyi is also a mother of two children, which makes her one of the most powerful moms in America!

On the Page and Screen

Many famous actors, writers, dancers, and film directors have immigrated to the United States. Salma Hayek was born in Mexico and moved to Los Angeles to study acting. Director Ang Lee, who was born in Taiwan, has won the Academy Award for Best Director for his films *Brokeback Mountain* and *Life of Pi*.

Here, Ang Lee appears onstage at the Cannes Film Festival, in France.

Edwidge Danticat
(1969–)

Edwidge Danticat is a Haitian American writer. She moved from Port-au-Prince, Haiti, to Brooklyn, New York, when she was 12. Her book *Breath, Eyes, Memory* is a story based on her immigration experience. Danticat speaks Haitian Creole, French, and English. She graduated from Brown University. She has taught creative writing at several colleges.

Khaled Hosseini, author of *The Kite Runner*, was born in Afghanistan. His family moved to France when he was 11, then applied for **asylum** in the United States four years later. Hosseini spoke no English when he arrived in California, but he later became a US citizen.

Salma Hayek's family is diverse. Her grandfather was Lebanese, and her mother's family has Spanish ancestors.

Serving in Government

Immigrants have held important positions and played roles in US politics. Madeleine Albright, who was born in the former Czechoslovakia and came to the United States at the age of 11, was the first woman to serve as secretary of state. The secretary of state serves as an advisor to the US president and is one of the highest-ranking officials in the US government.

Mazie Hirono, who serves as a US senator from Hawaii, was born in Japan to a mother who was a US citizen. She is the first Asian American woman elected to the Senate.

Carlos Gutierrez (1953–)

Carlos Gutierrez was born in Havana, Cuba. His family moved to Florida in 1960. Gutierrez was the US secretary of commerce under former president George W. Bush. The secretary of commerce works to help American businesses grow. Before that, Gutierrez was the head of Kellogg Company.

Madeleine Albright became a US citizen in 1957, when she was 20.

Sports Stars

Sports are another area where immigrants have made huge contributions. Robinson Canó, second baseman for the Seattle Mariners, was born in the Dominican Republic.

Patrick Ewing, who played basketball for the New York Knicks, came to the United States from Jamaica when he was 12. He is now in the Basketball Hall of Fame.

Robinson Canó (center) became a US citizen in 2012.

Martina Navratilova (1956–)

Martina Navratilova was born in Prague, Czechoslovakia, in 1956. She became a US citizen in 1981. Navratilova won the Wimbledon Ladies' Singles Championship six years in a row, from 1982 through 1987. She supports animal rights, gay and lesbian rights, and other political issues. Navratilova is in the International Tennis Hall of Fame.

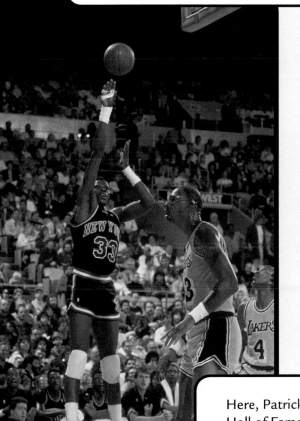

Another famous immigrant is Nadia Comaneci, who was born in Romania. Comaneci was the first female gymnast to get a perfect score in an Olympic event. In 1989, she **defected** to the United States and later became a US citizen.

Here, Patrick Ewing shoots over fellow Hall of Famer Kareem Abdul-Jabbar.

The American Mosaic

Throughout its history, the United States has been shaped by its immigrants. Immigrants have left their mark on art, music, food, sports, technology, and language. With this mix of cultures, the United States can be seen as a **mosaic**. A mosaic is a larger picture created by many smaller pieces.

Each person who lives in the United States is a different piece of the picture. As new immigrants continue to arrive, the picture continues to change!

Pop stars Rihanna (left) and Justin Bieber (right) are both immigrants. Rihanna was born in Barbados, while Bieber is from Canada.

Glossary

amended (uh-MEND-ed) Added or changed.

asylum (uh-SY-lum) Protection given by a country to persecuted people.

border (BOR-der) A dividing line between two places.

citizen (SIH-tih-zen) Someone who was born in or has a right to live in a country or other community.

contributions (kon-trih-BYOO-shunz) Things that are given.

culture (KUL-chur) The beliefs, practices, and arts of a group of people.

defected (dih-FEKT-ed) To have given up one's loyalty to one group or country to join another.

immigrants (IH-muh-grunts) People who move to a new country from another country.

mosaic (moh-ZAY-ik) A picture made by fitting together small pieces of stone, glass, or tile and pasting them in place.

permanent residents (PER-muh-nint REH-zuh-dents) People who are not citizens but who have the right to live and work in a country forever.

refugees (reh-fyoo-JEEZ) People who leave their own country to find safety.

technology (tek-NAH-luh-jee) Advanced tools that help people do and make things.

undocumented immigrants (un-DO-kyuh-men-ted IH-muh-grunts) People living in a country without the official paperwork that the law requires to let them do so.

Index

Websites

Due to the changing nature of Internet links, PowerKids Press has developed an online list of websites related to the subject of this book. This site is updated regularly. Please use this link to access the list:

www.powerkidslinks.com/mosa/famo/